# CAVALCADE

# NOEL COWARD

# Cavalcade

LONDON: WILLIAM HEINEMANN LTD

31981

FIRST PUBLISHED JANUARY 1932
REPRINTED SEPTEMBER 1932, MARCH 1933

PRINTED
IN GREAT BRITAIN
AT THE WINDMILL PRESS

TO

## G. B. STERN

DEAR PETER—

I am dedicating CAVALCADE to you in gratitude for a friendship maintained through many of its years.

NOEL.

# ILLUSTRATIONS

## SPEAKING PARTS

JANE MARRYOT
ROBERT MARRYOT
ELLEN
BRIDGES
EDWARD MARRYOT (small)
JOE MARRYOT
EDITH HARRIS
EDWARD (grown up)
JOE
EDITH
FANNY BRIDGES (small)
FANNY BRIDGES (grown up)
MARGARET HARRIS
MRS. SNAPPER
COOK
ANNIE
FLO GRAINGER
GEORGE GRAINGER
MIRABELLE
LIEUT. EDGAR
TOM JOLLY
ADA (Rose Darling)
DAISY DEVON
MARION CHRISTIE
NETTA LAKE (pianist)
CONNIE CRAWSHAY
TIM BATEMAN
DOUGLAS FINN
LORD MARTLET (Chubby)
1ST WOMAN
2ND WOMAN
UNCLE GEORGE
UNCLE DICK
GLADYS (parlourmaid)

## PART I

## PART II

## PART III

## NOTE ON PART I

In the interim of darkness between Scenes 1
and 2, 2 and 3, 3 and 4, newsboys are heard
shouting latest news from the front.

## SCENE I

*Principals*—1899

JANE MARRYOT (aged 31)
ROBERT MARRYOT (aged 33)
ELLEN (aged 25)
BRIDGES (aged 40)

8

MISS MARY CLARE AS "JANE MARRYOT."

# PART I

B

# SCENE I

SCENE: *The drawing-room of a London house. The room is charmingly furnished in the taste of the period. There are two windows at the back with a small balcony in front of each of them; apart from this structural necessity the decoration and furniture, etc., can be left to the discretion of the designer.*

TIME: *About 11.45 p.m. Sunday, December 31st, 1899.*

*When the curtain rises,* ELLEN, *the parlourmaid, is discovered setting the table with a light supper consisting of sandwiches and cake. She is a pleasant-looking woman of twenty-five.*

*Enter* BRIDGES, *the butler, with a bottle of champagne in a bucket of ice. He is older than* ELLEN, *about forty, with iron-grey hair.*

ELLEN: They won't need champagne if they've got 'ot punch, will they?

BRIDGES: You never know; best to be on the safe side.

ELLEN: How was Cook when you come up?

BRIDGES: Running round that kitchen like a cat on a griddle; New Year's Eve's gone to 'er 'ead, and no mistake.

ELLEN: She's been queer all day, she says she feels

3

like as if it was the end of everything. So do I, for that matter.

BRIDGES: Don't start all that over again.

ELLEN: Oh, Alfred!

BRIDGES: What?

ELLEN: I can't bear to think what it's going to be like when you've gone.

BRIDGES: Well, don't.

ELLEN: I can't 'elp it.

BRIDGES: It's no use upsetting yourself; think of the missus, think of all the other soldiers' wives. You're in the same boat as wot they are.

ELLEN: You was never cut out for a soldier.

BRIDGES: Never mind what I was cut out for. I am one now.

ELLEN: What's going to 'appen to me and Fanny if anything 'appens to you?

BRIDGES (*putting his hands on* ELLEN's *shoulders*): Look 'ere, old girl, you married me for better or for worse, didn't you?

ELLEN: Yes, but——

BRIDGES: Well, if this turns out to be worse, so much the worse, see? And if it turns out to be better——

ELLEN: So much the better—yes, a fat lot of comfort that is.

BRIDGES: Look at the Missus, with a brother out there ever since the beginning, and now 'er 'usband going, and two growing boys to look after.

ELLEN: What's the war for, anyhow? Nobody wanted to 'ave a war.

4

BRIDGES: We've got to 'ave wars every now and then to prove we're top-dog——

ELLEN: This one don't seem to be proving much.

BRIDGES: 'Ow can you tell sitting at 'ome 'ere safe and sound? 'Ow can you tell what our brave boys are suffering out there in darkest Africa, giving their life's blood for their Queen and country?

ELLEN: Africa looks very sunny and nice in the *Illustrated London News*.

BRIDGES: If this wasn't New Year's Eve, I'd lose my temper, and that's a fact.

ELLEN: Well, it wouldn't be the first time. You'd better go and get the 'ot punch, they'll be in in a minute.

BRIDGES: You mark my words, Ellen, if we didn't go out and give them Boers wot for, they'd be over 'ere wreakin' 'avoc and carnage before you could say Jack Robinson.

ELLEN: Oh, get along with you.

BRIDGES *goes out.*

ELLEN, *puts the finishing touches to the table and then, going to the windows, she pulls back the curtains.*

*Enter* JANE MARRYOT. *She is a handsome woman of about thirty-one. She is wearing an evening gown and cloak.*

*Enter* ROBERT, JANE's *husband, following her. He is older, about thirty-five, also in evening dress.*

JANE (*throwing off her cloak*): I thought we should never get here in time. I'm sure that cabby was tipsy, Robert. How nice the table looks, Ellen. Where did those flowers come from?

ELLEN: They're from Bridges and me, ma'am, with our very best wishes, I'm sure.

JANE: Thank you, Ellen, very much indeed.

ROBERT: A charming thought, Ellen. Thank you both.

ELLEN: Not at all, sir—it's—it's a pleasure indeed.

ELLEN *withdraws from the room covered with respectful embarrassment.*

JANE *smiles at* ROBERT.

JANE: Small things are so infinitely touching, aren't they? I feel I want to cry. Just a few gentle tears to usher in the new century.

ROBERT: Do, by all means, dearest: this evening was planned sentimentally.

JANE: Just the two of us saying, "Hail and Farewell."

ROBERT: Not farewell quite yet.

JANE: Soon—dreadfully soon.

ROBERT: You looked so beautiful at dinner.

JANE: Did I, Robert?

ROBERT: You look so beautiful now.

JANE: Do I, Robert?

ROBERT: I expect it's only that dress, really. Very deceiving.

JANE: Yes, Robert.

ROBERT: And that ornament in your hair.

JANE: Yes, Robert.

ROBERT: And the fact that I love you so dearly.

JANE: After so long. How can you?

ROBERT: Perhaps you're hideous and ill-dispositioned

6

and tedious, really, and I never knew.

JANE: Perhaps.

ROBERT: Well, it's too late now. I'm set in the habit of loving you. I shall never know the truth.

JANE: I wonder if the boys are asleep.

ROBERT: Snoring, I expect.

JANE: Oh, no, Robert; not snoring. They both have perfect tonsils. Doctor Harrison said so.

ROBERT: Inherited from their mother, dear. You have the most exquisite tonsils in the world.

JANE: You're in a very facetious mood, Robert. It shocks me a little. This should be a solemn occasion. Your bow is crooked, too, and you look raffish.

ROBERT: Raffish?

JANE (*suddenly running into his arms*): Oh, my darling, my darling, why must you leave me? I shall miss you so.

ROBERT (*smiling and holding her tenderly*): The Bugle Call, dear, the Red, White and Blue——

Britons never, never, never shall be slaves.

JANE: Don't tease me—not about that. What does it matter about the Boers—it can't matter, really.

ROBERT (*seriously*): It matters about Jim, doesn't it? He's out there.

JANE: Yes, I know, I know, but——

ROBERT: But what?

JANE (*leaving his embrace*): I'm sorry, dear. I was nearly behaving badly.

ROBERT: You couldn't behave badly.

JANE (*lightly*): Give him my love if you ever see him, if he's alive.

ROBERT: Of course he's alive. They're all alive. They're bound to be relieved soon.

JANE: Everyone has been saying that for weeks.

ROBERT: Baden Powell's a fine man.

JANE: How long will it last, the war, I mean?

ROBERT: It can't last more than a few months.

JANE: Perhaps it will be over before you get there.

ROBERT: Perhaps.

JANE: I suppose you'd hate that. Wouldn't you?

ROBERT: Bitterly.

JANE: Thank Heaven for one thing. The boys are too young. They won't have to fight; Peace and Happiness for them. Oh, please God, Peace and Happiness for them, always. (*She leans against the window and looks out.*)

> *Enter* BRIDGES *with a bowl of punch, followed by*:
> ELLEN *entering, carrying a tray of punch glasses and almonds and raisins.*

BRIDGES: It's started, sir. Just twelve o'clock now.

ROBERT: Open the windows quick.

> ROBERT *takes the punch from* BRIDGES *and fills two glasses.*
> BRIDGES *opens the windows wide.*
> *Outside can be heard the growing noise of sirens and chimes of bells.*
> ELLEN *and* BRIDGES *are about to go.*

JANE (*suddenly*): Stay and drink with us, won't you?

8

TOASTING THE NEW YEAR, DECEMBER, 1899.

Robert, two more glasses.

BRIDGES: Thank you very much, ma'am.

ELLEN: Thank you, ma'am.

ROBERT (*pouring them two glasses of punch*): Here you are, Jane, Ellen, Bridges. 1900—1900.

JANE: 1900.

ELLEN and BRIDGES (*together*): 1900.

> *Suddenly* JANE *hears a sound upstairs. She puts down her glass hurriedly and:*
>
> JANE *runs out of the room.*

ELLEN: It sounded like Master Joe.

ROBERT (*going to the door and calling after* JANE): Dearest, bring them down here. Bring them both down. (*Coming slowly back into the room, smiling*) How very impolite of the twentieth century to waken the children.

> *The lights fade as the noise of chimes and sirens grows louder.*

# SCENE  II

*Principals*

ROBERT
JANE
ELLEN
BRIDGES

*Illustrated London News*

THE "C.I.V.'s" MARCH TO WAR.

THE DEPARTURE OF THE TROOPSHIP.

# SCENE II

> *Before the stage becomes visible to the audience, down*
> *stage on the left* BRIDGES *and* ELLEN *appear in a pool*
> *of light.* BRIDGES *is wearing the uniform of a Private*
> *in the C.I.V.* ELLEN *is gaily dressed, but weeping.*

BRIDGES: Be brave, old woman.

ELLEN: Oh, Alfred, Alfred, my 'eart's breaking.

BRIDGES: There, there—I'll soon be back—you see.

ELLEN: I can't bear it.

BRIDGES: Think of the missus—you'll 'ave to look after 'er, you know.

ELLEN: I can't think of anything but you going out among all them awful Boers and lying bleeding yer 'eart out on the battlefield.

BRIDGES: That's a cheerful outlook, I will say.

ELLEN: And Fanny 'aving no father and me being widowed for life.

BRIDGES: You're getting morbid, you know. Fanny'll be all right, and so will you and so will I. She was right as rain when I kissed her good-bye. See her laugh, eh?

ELLEN: She didn't mean to laugh; she's too young to understand.

BRIDGES: All the better, I say. I could do with a bit

of a smile from you, now you mention it.

ELLEN: All right—I'll try.

BRIDGES: That's a girl—— (*He kisses her as*):

> *The lights fade on them and a steamer siren sounds loudly.*
>
> *Down stage on the right* ROBERT *and* JANE *appear in a pool of light.*
>
> ROBERT *is in the uniform of a C.I.V. officer.*
>
> JANE *is quietly dressed.*

ROBERT: I think I'd better be getting aboard.

JANE: It's come at last, hasn't it—this moment?

ROBERT: You'll be very brave, won't you?

JANE: Take care of yourself, my dearest.

ROBERT: I shall probably be seasick.

JANE: Lie down flat on every possible occasion.

ROBERT: I'll try to remember.

JANE: Bridges will look after you.

ROBERT: Perhaps he'll be lying down flat, too.

JANE: You mustn't worry about me being unhappy when you've gone. I'm going to keep myself very busy. Lady Brandon is organizing an enormous relief fund matinée in February. She asked me to help her, and there'll be lots of other things, too. I shan't give myself time to feel anything except just very proud.

ROBERT: I'll write and telegraph whenever it's possible.

> *Pause.*

JANE: This is horrid, isn't it?

ROBERT: I really must go.

JANE: Not just for a minute.

ROBERT: I'm going to kiss you once more now, and then I want you to turn away and go on talking, so that you won't see me actually leave you.

JANE (*in a stifled voice*): Very well, my darling.

ROBERT *kisses her lingeringly.*

(*Turning away and talking rapidly*): Edward and Joe were terribly anxious to come, too, but I'm glad I didn't bring them really. Joe gets over-excited so easily, and he's had a very bad cold, anyhow. Edward could have come, I suppose, really, but that would have upset Joe so dreadfully, being left alone. Take care of yourself, my own dear—you're not here any more, so I can break down a little—I felt you go when I said about Joe being over-excited—Robert—Robert——

ROBERT *has disappeared into the surrounding darkness. As she turns the lights go up and* ROBERT *is seen threading his way through the crowd to the ship's gangway.* BRIDGES *is waiting for him, and they go aboard together.* JANE *walks over to* ELLEN, *who is sobbing bitterly, and puts her arms round her. The crowd is cheering wildly, although several mothers and sweethearts and wives are weeping.*

*The steamer gives a short blast on its siren.*

*A band strikes up "Soldiers of the Queen."*

*The decks of the ship are lined with waving soldiers.*

*The gangway is pulled away. Slowly the ship begins to move as:*

*The lights fade.*

15

# SCENE III

*Principals*

JANE MARRYOT
MARGARET HARRIS
EDITH HARRIS (aged 10)
EDWARD (aged 12)
JOE (aged 8)
ELLEN

C

# SCENE III

SCENE: *The same as* SCENE I.

TIME: *About five o'clock on the afternoon of Friday, May 18th, 1900.*

*When the lights go up* EDWARD *and* JOE MARRYOT *and* EDITH HARRIS *are discovered playing soldiers on the floor.* EDWARD *is aged twelve,* JOE *eight, and* EDITH HARRIS *about ten.*

JOE (*shooting off a cannon*): Bang—bang, bang, bang.

EDITH (*giving a little squeak*): Oh—oh, dear!

EDWARD: How many?

EDITH: Seven.

EDWARD (*curtly*): Good! You'd better retreat.

EDITH: I don't know how.

JOE: I'm going to shoot again.

EDITH: I do wish you wouldn't. I've only got fourteen left.

JOE (*yelling*): Bang, bang, bang! Dirty old Kruger—dirty old Kruger——

EDWARD: Shut up! How dare you fire without orders.

JOE (*saluting*): I'm sorry, Bobs.

EDITH: Edward.

EDWARD: What?

EDITH: Need I always be the Boers?

EDWARD: Yes.

EDITH: Why?

JOE: Because you're a girl—only a girl. Bang, bang, bang!

EDITH (*struggling with her cannon and ammunition*): I'll teach you, you mean little pig! Bang, bang, bang! There! Bang——

> *The cannon sticks, so* EDITH *throws it at* JOE's *battalion, annihilating about fifty soldiers.*

JOE (*yelling*): It's not fair.

EDWARD: Be quiet. Edith, that was cheating.

EDITH (*in tears*): I'm sick of being the Boers—I'll never be the Boers again, never as long as I live!

> *The door opens.*
>
> *Enter* JANE, *looking obviously worried and nervy.*
>
> *Enter* MARGARET HARRIS, *following* JANE. *She is a nicely dressed woman of about thirty.*

JANE: Children, why on earth are you making such an awful noise? I heard you right down in the hall. Edith, what's the matter? Joe be quiet.

EDWARD: Edith doesn't like being the Boers—she's mutinied.

JANE: So I should think.

JOE: Bang, bang, bang!

> JOE *throws* EDITH's *cannon back at her and hits her on the knee.*
>
> EDITH *screams.*
>
> JANE *slaps* JOE *sharply.*

JANE: You're a naughty, wicked, little boy. You go upstairs this minute.

> MARGARET *rushes to* EDITH *and proceeds to comfort her.*

20

MARGARET: Edith, don't cry—it couldn't have hurt you so very much.

JANE: I can't bear it. Go away, all of you. Edward, take Joe away.

EDWARD: Sorry, mum.

JANE: Can't you play any other game but soldiers, soldiers—soldiers hurting each other—killing each other? Go away from me—go away—go away—go away——

MARGARET, *seeing that* JANE *is in a bad state of nerves, bustles all three children out of the room.*

MARGARET: Go along, all of you. Edith, I'm ashamed of you, making such a fuss. It's only a tiny little scratch. Go upstairs and ask nurse to put some Pommade Devigne on it. Go along, now.

*Exeunt* EDITH, EDWARD *and* JOE.

MARGARET *shuts the door after the children and comes back to* JANE.

JANE *is wearily removing her hat in front of a mirror.*

*A barrel organ in the street strikes up "Soldiers of the Queen."*

JANE: There's no escape anywhere, is there?

MARGARET: Shall I throw him something?

JANE: Make him go away.

MARGARET *goes to the window and out on to the balcony.*

MARGARET: Hi! Hi!

*The organ stops.*

Will you please go away further down the street?

(*Throwing some money out and returning into the room*) He's moving off. Do sit down, Jane dear, you've been standing up all the afternoon.

JANE (*sitting down*): Will these days never end?

*The barrel organ starts again, but much further off.*

MARGARET: News will come soon.

JANE: I don't believe I shall see either of them ever again.

MARGARET: Don't give way to despair, Jane. It's foolish. You must have courage.

JANE: It's much easier to be brave when there's something to hear, something definite; this long suspense, these dragging, dragging weeks of waiting are horrible. The two people I love best in the world, so remote from me, beyond reach of my love, probably suffering—it's dreadful, dreadful——

MARGARET: Mafeking is bound to be relieved within the next few days, all the papers say so.

JANE: They've been saying so for months—meanwhile Jim is dying there slowly, by inches, starvation and disease and horror. I can't bear to think of it and yet I can't stop thinking. I wake at night and see his face, as he was when he was a little boy. He was always awfully plucky, my little brother, and so very, very dear to me. (*She breaks down.*)

*Enter* ELLEN *with tea. She places it on the table and looks enquiringly at* MARGARET.

MARGARET *shakes her head.*

MARGARET: No news yet, Ellen. We've been standing outside the Mansion House for hours, and then we went to Fleet Street to the newspaper offices.

ELLEN (*to* JANE): Have a nice cup of tea, ma'am, it'll make you feel better.

JANE: Thank you, Ellen.

ELLEN: There ain't no cause to worry about the master, ma'am; he's all right. I feel it in me bones. You see, he's got my Alfred with 'im, and if anything 'appened to either of them we'd be bound to 'ear from one of them, if you know what I mean.

JANE: You must be fearfully worried, too, Ellen.

ELLEN: Well, on and off, I am, but I say to myself— no news is good news, and what must be must be, and you'd never believe how it cheers me up.

> ELLEN *goes out.*

MARGARET: Poor Ellen!

> *A newsboy runs by, shouting.*

JANE (*jumping up*): Quick! Quick! Give me a halfpenny.

> JANE *rushes on to the balcony and leans over.*

What is it, Ellen—what is it?

> ELLEN *apparently answers "nothing much," and*
> JANE *returns wearily.*

Ellen's up those area steps like lightning every time a paper boy passes. No news is good news. What must be must be. Oh, God!

> MARGARET *gets up with an air of determination.*

MARGARET: Now, look here, Jane. I'm going now, and I shall be back at a quarter to seven.

JANE: A quarter to seven—why?

MARGARET: We're going out to dine at a restaurant

and we're going to a theatre.

JANE: A restaurant! A theatre! I couldn't!

MARGARET: You could and you will—it's senseless sitting at home all by yourself fretting and worrying, and it doesn't do any good. I'll get Ronnie James to take us, and if he can't, we'll go by ourselves, and I don't care what people say. We'll go to something gay —they say "Mirabelle" is very good.

JANE: I can't Margaret—it's very sweet of you, but I really can't.

MARGARET: I am now going home to have a bath and put on my new Redfern model, and I shall be back at a quarter to seven.

JANE: Margaret—no, really, I——

MARGARET (*kissing* JANE): Don't argue—just do what you're told.

JANE: I haven't anything to wear.

MARGARET: Nonsense! You have your blue "Worth" and if that won't do, put on your presentation gown, feathers and all!

JANE: Margaret, don't be so silly.

MARGARET: I mean it—it's a gesture. Robert and Jim would hate to think of you weeping and wailing. They're being gallant enough. We'd better try and be gallant, too. We'll dine at the Café Royal.

JANE: Margaret!

MARGARET: Be ready at a quarter to seven.

MARGARET *goes out.*

JANE *makes a movement to call* MARGARET *back and then subsides into her chair.*

24

*Suddenly directly under the window another barrel organ strikes up "Soldiers of the Queen."*

JANE *jumps up and runs to the window.*

JANE (*on balcony*): Go on, then—play louder—play louder! Soldiers of the Queen—wounded and dying and suffering for the Queen! Play louder, play louder!

*She comes back into the room laughing hysterically and proceeds to kick the children's toy soldiers all over the room; finally collapsing on to the sofa in a storm of tears as:*

*The lights fade.*

## SCENE IV

*Principals*

JANE
MARGARET
MIRABELLE
ADA
EDGAR
TOM JOLLY
SIX C.I.V. GIRLS
CHORUS
STAGE MANAGER

# SCENE IV

SCENE: *A theatre.*

TIME: *About 9 p.m. Friday, May 18th, 1900.*

*Before the lights go up, a spotlight illuminates* JANE *and* MARGARET *in evening cloaks and gowns sitting in a stage box left. When the lights go up, it is seen that they are watching a typical musical comedy of the period.*

*A Sextette of ample girls are singing a song called "The Girls of the C.I.V.", dressed rakishly in C.I.V. uniforms.*

We're the girls of the C.I.V.
Form fours, get in line, one two three.
For our bravery is such
That the Boers won't like it much
When we chase them across the veldt and
    teach them double Dutch
We're the girls of the C.I.V.
And we're out for a lark and a spree
In our uniforms so stunning
We shall soon have Kruger running
From the girls of the C.I.V.

*The Scene on the stage is excessively rural, with apple blossom predominating. When the girls have finished*

29

*their number, they bounce off and:*

*The leading lady,* MIRABELLE, *enters. She is in reality a Princess, but has disguised herself as a farm girl in order that she might conceivably find a young man to love her for herself alone. Her costume is charming but slightly inappropriate for manual labour.*

*She is met down stage by* LIEUT. EDGAR TYRELL, R.N., *a wooden young man with an excellent tenor voice.*

EDGAR (*saluting*): We meet again.

MIRABELLE (*curtseying*): Yes, indeed.

EDGAR: It seems a sin that beauty so rare should be hidden for ever in this small country village.

MIRABELLE: Flatterer!

EDGAR: No, no, I mean it.

MIRABELLE: You are a sailor, sir, and I have been warned about sailors.

EDGAR: What have they told you?

MIRABELLE: That sailors are fickle, and that when they have loved a maid they sail away and leave her lonely.

EDGAR: Do you believe that?

MIRABELLE: I hardly know.

EDGAR: Dearest, dearest Mirabelle—my heart is at your feet.

MIRABELLE (*gaily*): Pick it up, sir, pick it up.

EDGAR: Ah, do not tease me. Look into my eyes— can you not see the lovelight shining there?

MIRABELLE: I know nothing of love.

EDGAR: Let me teach you.

MIRABELLE: I know nothing of life.

*Daily Mail Photo*

MISS STRELLA WILSON AS "MIRABELLE."

## MIRABELLE WALTZ

LOVER OF MY DREAMS

SHE:  A simple country maid am I,
      As innocent as any flower.
      The great big world has pass'd me by,
      No lover comes my way to greet me shyly in
          my bower.
HE:   Oh, say not so!
      Such modesty enchants me:
      Could I but stay to while away with you a happy
          hour.
SHE:  It must be Spring that fills my heart to over-
          flowing,
      Ah, whither am I going?
      What is the voice that seems to say:
      Be kind to love, don't let him call to you
          unknowing.
HE:   If true love comes to you don't turn your face
          away.
SHE:  Maybe 'tis something in the air;
      For Spring is made for lovers only.
HE:   Live for the moment and take care
      Lest love should fly and leave us lonely.
BOTH: Ah, if love should leave us lonely.

REFRAIN

SHE:  All my life I have been waiting
      Dreaming ages through;
      Until to-day I suddenly discover

31

The form and face of he who is my lover.
No more tears and hesitating
Fate has sent me you
Time and tide can never sever
Those whom love has bound forever,
Dear Lover of my Dreams come true.

HE:     All my life I have been waiting,
SHE:    All my life I have been waiting,
HE:     Dreaming ages through;
SHE:    Dreaming ages through;
HE:     Until to-day I suddenly discover
SHE:    Until to-day I suddenly discover
HE:     The form and face of she who is my lover.
SHE:    The form and face of he who is my lover.
HE:     No more tears and hesitating;
SHE:    No more tears and hesitating;
HE:     Fate has sent me you—Time and tide can never
        sever,
SHE:    Fate has sent me you and tide can never sever
HE:     Those whom love has bound for ever,
SHE:    Those whom love has bound for ever,
HE:     Dear lover of my Dreams come true,
SHE:    Dear lover of my Dreams come true,
BOTH:   Dear lover of my
        Dreams come true,
        Dear lover of my Dreams come true,
        Dear lover of my Dreams come true.

*Enter* TOM JOLLY, *comedian. He is dressed as a common sailor.*

*Enter* ADA *with* TOM (*soubrette*). *She is dressed as a dairymaid.*

TOM: If I make a noise like a cow—would you kiss me?

ADA (*laughing*): Perhaps.

TOM: Moo—moo. (*He tries to kiss her.*)

ADA: No, no! I'm frightened of bulls.

TOM: If I make a noise like a sheep—then?

ADA: Who knows!

TOM: Baa, baa, baa——

ADA: No, no—no good at all.

TOM: I'll sing, then. Sailing, sailing, over the bounding main!

ADA: I'll kiss you now. I love donkeys!


## FUN OF THE FARM

### VERSE

ADA:    Tho' sailors are so brave and bold,
        It really must be dreadfully cold
           To sail across the sea.

TOM:        I quite agree,
           I quite agree,
        I'm sick of the ocean wild and free,
        Heigho, heigho, this is the place for me.

ADA:    Now I am weary of the town
        And feel inclined to settle down
           A milk pail on my arm.

TOM:        I feel afraid,
            A London maid
Would never know how the eggs are laid.

ADA:    I'd find a cow
            And milk 'til the pail was full,

TOM:    I'd shear the sow
            And probably milk the bull.

BOTH:           You must agree
                That it would be
The height of true rusticity
If you and I should settle on a farm.

REFRAIN

BOTH: Oh, the Fun of the Farmyard,
                The roosters are crowing,
                The cattle are lowing,
The turkeys go gobbly gobbly goo;
This really is an alarm yard.

ADA:            Like little Bo-Peep,
                I lose my sheep,
And cannot find them anywhere.

TOM:            I ought to be shot,
                For I forgot
To coax the horse to meet the mare.

BOTH:           Who left the canary
                Locked up in the dairy?

ADA:        Cheep, cheep, cheep, cheep,

TOM:        Snort, snort, snort, snort,

ADA:        Moo, moo, moo, moo,

TOM:        Cock a doodle doodle do!

34

BOTH:        Oh, dear, far from being a calm yard,
             Quack, quack, quack, quack,
                All the fun of the farm.

TOM: Tell me something, Ada.
ADA: What?
TOM: You're no dairymaid, are you?
ADA: Mr. Inquisitive.
TOM: What are you?
ADA (*curtseying*): Lady's maid to the Princess
Mirabelle.
        MIRABELLE *enters unobserved at the back.*
TOM: The Princess! Then he'll win his bet, after all.
ADA: Who? What bet?
TOM: Lieutenant Edgar. All the officers of the ship
wagered him that he would not win the hand of the
Princess Mirabelle. He said he'd marry her if she was
ugly as sin; he needs the money.
        EDGAR *enters.*
EDGAR: What are you doing here, Tom?
TOM: Just farming! (*Laugh.*)
MIRABELLE: Stop!
        *Enter full* CHORUS.


## FINALE

CHORUS:      What is—what is the matter here?
MIRABELLE:   Kind friends, you heard my call,
             And so I thank you all
             For while you chatter here
             My heart has been betrayed.

EDGAR:      Ah, no—not so.
            What foolish words you scatter here.
            'Tis naught but your pride that's hurt
            I am afraid.
CHORUS:     Who can he be,
            'Tis plain to see,
                He seems to know her well.
            Who is this man
            Who dares offend
                The Princess Mirabelle?
MIRABELLE:  You've lied to me and cheated me.
ADA:        Madame, don't let him see
            Your poor heart breaking.
EDGAR:      What ere the future be,
            True love you are mistaking.


### WALTZ REFRAIN FINALE


            All my life I have been dreaming,
            Now my dreams must die.
            Within my heart I felt a song awaken,
            And now I find a melody forsaken.
            All your vows were base and scheming,
            All our Love's a lie.
            Cruelly you would deceive me,
            All I say to you is . . .

   *Enter* STAGE MANAGER, *who raises his hand for
silence.*

36

*The Graphic*

MAFEKING NIGHT IN TRAFALGAR SQUARE.

STAGE MANAGER: Ladies and gentlemen—Mafeking has been relieved.

JANE *in her box utters a cry of relief.*

*The players on the stage cheer wildly and the lights fade.*

*The cheering is heard through the darkness; when the lights come up the audience is discovered cheering, waving hats and handkerchiefs, and programmes are fluttering from the crowded balconies; some of the audience join hands and sing "Auld Lang Syne." The lights fade.*

# SCENE V

*Principals*

MRS. SNAPPER
COOK
ANNIE
ELLEN
BRIDGES
CABBY

BRIDGES COMES HOME FROM THE SOUTH AFRICAN WAR.

## SCENE V

SCENE: *The kitchen of a London house. It is a typical basement kitchen. There is a door at the back opening on to the area steps, also two windows. Another door communicating with the upper parts of the house, and a small door leading into the scullery.*

TIME: *About 5 p.m. Monday, January 21st, 1901.*

*When the lights go up* COOK *is making toast in front of the range.*

MRS. SNAPPER (ELLEN'S *Mother*) *is sitting on a chair beside a mail-cart in which reposes (mercifully invisible to the audience) the infant* FANNY.

ANNIE, *a scullery-maid, stands about with her mouth open, obviously in a state of considerable excitement, occasionally putting ineffective finishing touches to the table.*

COOK: 'Ere, Annie, 'old this fork a minute, or we'll have to call the Fire Brigade to put my face out.

ANNIE *takes the fork.*

COOK *fans herself with her apron.*

MRS. S.: I once knew a woman whose front 'air caught fire when she was making toast, and before you could count ten the 'ole room was ablaze. They'd never 'ave been able to recognize her remains if it 'adn't been for 'er cameo brooch.

COOK: They must 'ave known who she was. (*Coming over to the mail-cart*) And 'ow's her ladyship—who's a lovely girl, eh? Don't burn that toast, Annie. (*She clicks her tongue at the infant* FANNY.) Yer dad's comin' 'ome, ducks, safe and sound. (*She chants in order to entertain* FANNY.) Safe and sound, safe and sound.

MRS. S.: I only 'ope 'e is safe and sound, I'm sure.

COOK: The telegram said 'e was.

MRS. S.: Maybe it was a lie to spare Ellen's feelings.

COOK: You're a cheerful one, I must say.

MRS. S.: When I was a girl a friend of mine's 'usband come back unexpected from the Crimea with no legs at all.

*This is too much for* ANNIE, *who drops the toast and goes off into snuffles of laughter.*

COOK: Stop it, Annie—now look what you've done—cut another piece, quick, they'll be 'ere in a minute.

MRS. S.: I do 'ope Ellen didn't cry at the station, it does make her nose so red.

COOK: Alfred will be so pleased to see 'er 'e won't mind if it's red or blue. Come on, Annie, 'urry.

ANNIE: 'Ere they are.

COOK: 'Ere, quick! The rosette for baby. (*She rushes to the dresser and snatches up a red, white and blue rosette.*) You pin it on 'er, Mrs. Snapper, while I tidy me 'air.

ANNIE (*at window*): They've come in a cab. Oo-er!

*There is a great air of tension and excitement in the*

42

*kitchen, while* ELLEN'S *and* BRIDGES' *legs appear down the area steps.*

*The* CABBY *follows with* BRIDGES' *kit-bag, which is dumped in the passage.*

BRIDGES *enters first, looking very hale and hearty.*

BRIDGES (*entering*): You settle the cab, Ellen, I want to see my love-a-duck. 'Allo, Cook—'allo, Ma—where's my girl?

*He kisses* COOK *and* MRS. SNAPPER, *and then puts his head inside the pram.*

'Allo, Fanny. Coo, 'aven't you grown. Ma, you 'aven't 'arf bin feedin' 'er up. (*He makes delighted gurgling noises and prods the baby with his finger.*) See 'er laugh—she knows 'er dad.

*He puts his head inside again apparently kissing her heartily.*

ELLEN *comes in flushed and happy.*

ELLEN: I thought that train would never come—an whole hour I waited—an' all the people yellin' and screamin'. 'Ere, Alfred, take yer great 'ead out of that pram, you'll frighten 'er.

BRIDGES (*withdrawing*): She knows me, that's wot—she knows 'er old dad. Look at 'er rosette and all, smart as my eye. (*He turns and sees* ANNIE.) 'Ere, who's this? We 'aven't 'ad the pleasure.

ELLEN: This is Annie.

BRIDGES: 'Ullo, Annie.

ANNIE (*giggling*): Welcome 'ome, Mr. Bridges.

ANNIE *and* BRIDGES *shake hands.*

BRIDGES (*putting his arm round* MRS. SNAPPER):

43

Well, Ma, 'ow's everything?

MRS. S.: I mustn't grumble.

BRIDGES: So I should just think not. I got a surprise for you.

MRS. S.: What is it?

BRIDGES: Ellen knows; I told 'er in the cab. Tell 'er, Ellen.

ELLEN: No, you. Go on.

BRIDGES: Well, you know I said in my letters about a lad called Smart—'Erbert Smart.

COOK: Yes. Ellen read your letters aloud.

BRIDGES: Not all of 'em, I 'ope.

ELLEN: Get on with you, you never let yourself go further than a P.S. and a couple of crosses.

BRIDGES: Well, 'Erbert Smart's got a pub, see, and he's staying out in Africa, and I've bought it from 'im cheap, see? So much a year until it's paid off. We always wanted to 'ave somewhere of our own, and you can come and live with us, Ma—'ow's that suit?

MRS. S.: A pub—is it a respectable pub?

BRIDGES: All depends 'ow you behave, Ma, you know what you are when you've 'ad a couple.

MRS. S. (*sniggering*): Oh, Alfred, 'ow can you?

BRIDGES: Well, what d'you think about it?

MRS. S.: It sounds lovely—but 'ow about them upstairs?

BRIDGES: That's all right. I took the master into me confidence. He wished me luck.

MRS. S. (*breaking down*): Oh, dear, I can 'ardly believe it, not 'aving to live alone any more—oh, dear!

44

BRIDGES: 'Ere, cheer up, Ma. Come on, 'ave a cup of tea. There ain't nothing to cry about. Let's all 'ave tea, for God's sake. Come on, Cook, me old girl— 'ow'd you like to be a barmaid, eh?

> *They all sit down to tea, a grand tea with eggs and shrimps. Everybody is talking at once.*
>
> *Suddenly the cry of a* NEWSBOY *outside cuts through their conversation.*

BRIDGES: What's 'e yelling about?

COOK (*giving* ANNIE *a halfpenny*): 'Ere, Annie, go and get one, quick.

> ANNIE *runs out of the area steps.*
>
> *There is silence in the kitchen.*

BRIDGES: What's up? What's the matter?

ELLEN: It isn't anything to concern us.

COOK: Ellen, 'ow can you—it concerns the whole country.

> ANNIE *comes clattering back with the paper.*
>
> BRIDGES *snatches paper from* ANNIE *and reads it.*

BRIDGES (*reading*): Whew! The Queen—it says she's sinking!

MRS. S.: There now—I told you so.

COOK (*taking paper*): Let's 'ave a look.

ANNIE: She's very old, ain't she?

COOK: Be quiet, Annie. What's that got to do with it?

ANNIE: Well, I never seen 'er.

BRIDGES: I 'ave—driving along Birdcage Walk once —years ago. Coo! England won't 'arf seem funny without the Queen!

> *The lights fade out.*

45

*Stage Photo Company*

IN KENSINGTON GARDENS: THE QUEEN IS DEAD.

## SCENE VI

*Principals*

ROBERT
JANE
MARGARET
EDITH
EDWARD
JOE

# SCENE VI

SCENE: *Kensington Gardens. There is a row of high railings down stage so that the audience can see through them the trees and shrubs and seats and people and dogs.*
TIME: *About noon, Sunday, January 27th, 1901.*

*During the course of this scene there should be no word spoken. Everyone is in black and they walk slowly as though perpetually conscious of the country's mourning. Even the children are in black and one* WOMAN *leading a large brown dog has tied an enormous black crepe bow on to his collar.*

ROBERT *and* JANE *walk slowly from the left, followed by* EDWARD *and* JOE.

MARGARET HARRIS *and* EDITH *come from right.*

*They all meet and carry on a subdued conversation for a moment centre, and then part and go their different ways as:*

*The lights fade on the scene.*

## SCENE VII

*Principals*

JANE
MARGARET
EDWARD
JOE
EDITH
ELLEN
BRIDGES
COOK
ANNIE

# SCENE VII

SCENE: *Drawing-room of a London House.*
TIME: *About noon, Saturday, February 2nd,* 1901.

> *When the lights go up, the children,* EDWARD, JOE
> *and* EDITH, *all in black, are discovered out on the
> balcony.*
> MARGARET *and* JANE *are seated on the sofa.*
> *There is a small table beside* MARGARET *and* JANE
> *on which there is hot cocoa and cake.*

JOE (*on balcony*): Mum, mum, there's a policeman on a
lovely white horse!

JANE: Don't jump about, darling, and get hot and
excited. Edward, keep Joe as quiet as possible.

EDWARD: All right, mum.

JANE: More cocoa, Margaret?

MARGARET: No, thank you, dear.

JANE: I feel listless and sad, as though her death were
a personal grief. Strange, isn't it?

MARGARET: I think everyone feels that. (*She rises and
goes to the window.*) All those crowds and crowds of
people; they've been waiting for hours so patient and
quiet. There's hardly a sound.

JOE (*running in*): Mum, could I ever be a policeman?

JANE: Perhaps, darling—if you're good.

JOE: Are all policemen good?

JANE: Yes, dear, as good as gold.

JOE: Why did Queen Victoria die, mum?

JANE: Because she was a very old lady, and very tired.

JOE: Could I have another piece of cake?

JANE: You won't be able to eat any luncheon.

JOE: I'd rather have the cake.

JANE (*smiling*): Very well, then—a small piece. Take some out to Edward and Edith.

JOE: Thanks, mum.

> JOE *dashes out on to the balcony with the cake.*

MARGARET: How proud you must feel, Jane. All your troubles are over—Robert's home, Jim's home. Robert has a V.C.

JANE: Jim ought to have a V.C. too. All those dreadful months.

EDWARD (*rushing in*): They're coming! They're coming! Quick—quick!

JANE (*rising*): Run and fetch Ellen and Bridges and Cook.

> EDWARD *tears out of the room.*
> JOE *rushes in.*

JOE: Mum, please come out. I dropped a bit of cake. I couldn't help it—Edward pushed me.

> JANE *goes out and looks over.*
> *An intelligible voice is heard below.*

JANE (*leaning over*): I'm very sorry, it was an accident.

> *The voice mumbles something.*

He didn't throw it—he dropped it. It was an accident.

THE FUNERAL OF QUEEN VICTORIA: KING EDWARD
AND THE KAISER IN THE FOREGROUND.

(*She comes in again.*) Did you throw it, Joe, on purpose?
        JOE *hangs his head.*
You're a very naughty little boy indeed, and I've a very
good mind not to let you see the procession at all.
        EDITH *comes in.*
        *Following* EDITH *are* EDWARD, ELLEN, BRIDGES,
        COOK *and* ANNIE, *very smartened up.*
        EDWARD: Mum, will father be riding in the beginning
part or the end part?
        JANE: The beginning, I think.  Cook, you'd better
come out here, Annie, too.  Ellen, look after them, will
you?  Bridges, oughtn't you to be wearing a coat, it's
very cold?
        BRIDGES: I'm all right, thank you, ma'am.  Warm as
toast.
        EDWARD (*on balcony*): Here they come—quickly,
mum!
        *Everybody crowds out on to the two balconies.*
        *There is dead silence and then far away the solemn
        music of the Dead March is heard.  As it draws nearer
        the children jump about excitedly.*
        JOE (*suddenly*): Look, look—there's father—there's
father!
        JANE: Shhh! Joe, be quiet—keep still.
        *The procession continues.  Suddenly there is an
        outburst of cheering from the crowd which is instantly
        subdued.*
That's Lord Roberts.  He held up his hand to stop
them cheering.
        JOE: Is that Bobs, mum—is that Bobs?

EDWARD: Look, look—one-armed Giffard. Oh, mother, look——

JANE: Shhh! Now then, Joe, Edward, stand absolutely still—to attention, like father showed you.

*The* BOYS *stand rigid with their hands to their sides.*

*BRIDGES stands rigid with his hands to his side, on the other balcony.*

*The music swells as the band passes directly underneath them. As it begins to die away* COOK *bursts into tears.*

JANE: Five kings riding behind her.

JOE: Mum, she must have been a very little lady.

*The lights fade.*

A SCENE SHOWING THE FULL SPLENDOUR OF A TYPICAL
EDWARDIAN BALL.

# SCENE VIII

*Principals*

ROBERT
JANE
DUCHESS OF CHURT
MAJOR DOMO

THE FAMOUS "EMPIRE PROMENADE" IN 1902.
(From an illustration in G. R. Sims' "Living London.")

# SCENE VIII

SCENE: *The Grand Staircase of a London house. The head of the staircase is down stage. The stairs descending downwards and out of sight. Behind the well of the staircase, can be seen between columns, the beautifully decorated ballroom in which an orchestra is playing the popular waltzes of the day and people are dancing. The Ball is in full swing.*

TIME: *About 11 p.m. Thursday, May 14th, 1903.*

*When the lights go up, the full splendour of a typical Edwardian Ball should, if possible, burst upon the audience.*

*On the right and left of the staircase a balustraded balcony leads to the ballroom at the entrance of which* FOOTMEN *stand with programmes to hand to the guests.*

*The* DUCHESS OF CHURT *stands near the head of the stairs.*

*Near the* DUCHESS OF CHURT *stands the* MAJOR DOMO, *who announces each guest in stentorian tones.*

*There is a steady babel of conversation and music, but above it all can be heard the names of guests as they are announced. One by one, or sometimes escorted, come the great beauties of the day. They are all received by the* DUCHESS *and then make their way towards the ballroom. Finally the* MAJOR DOMO *announces:* "SIR ROBERT *and* LADY MARRYOT" *and:*

59

ROBERT *and* JANE *appear,* ROBERT *with full decorations, and* JANE *in an elaborate ball gown. As they are received by their hostess:*
*The lights fade and the curtain falls.*

END OF PART I

# PART II

# SCENE I

*Principals*

JANE
EDWARD (aged 18)
ELLEN
FANNY (aged 7)
MRS. SNAPPER
GEORGE
FLO
BRIDGES

# SCENE I

SCENE: *The Bar Parlour of a London pub.*
TIME: *About 5 p.m. Saturday, June 16th, 1906.*

> *When the curtain rises High Tea is just over. Seated round the table are* JANE, EDWARD, MRS. SNAPPER, FLO *and* GEORGE GRAINGER. FLO *and* GEORGE *are very smartly got up.* ELLEN *is seated at the piano with her back to the room.* FANNY (*aged* 7) *is dancing. When the dance is finished everyone applauds.*

JANE: She dances beautifully. Ellen. Come here, dear.
> FANNY *goes to her.*
I knew you when you were a little tiny baby.

FLO: She's a born dancer, if you ask me—haighly talented, haighly.

ELLEN (*leaving the piano*): She certainly does love it. On the go all day she is, jigging about.

MRS. S.: Can I press you to another cup, your ladyship?

JANE: No, thank you, we really must be going in a moment.

FLO (*to* EDWARD): 'Ow was Hoxford when you left it, Mr. Marryott?

EDWARD: Awfully nice.

FLO: I've never been there mayself, but George 'as, haven't you, George?

GEORGE: Oh, yes, nice place, Oxford. Very antique
—if you know what I mean.

ELLEN: I'm so glad to 'ear the master, Sir Robert, is
well.

JANE: He was so sorry not to be able to come down,
but as you know, he's a very busy man these days. He
wished very specially to be remembered to you and
your husband. He'll be sorry to hear that he's ill.

GEORGE: Ill! Alf ill! What's wrong with him?

MRS. SNAPPER *nudges* GEORGE *violently.*

ELLEN *speaks hurriedly.*

ELLEN: Before you and Flo come, George, I was
explaining to 'er Ladyship about poor Alfred's bad leg.

GEORGE: Bad leg?

MRS. S. (*frowning at* GEORGE): Yes, very bad—'e's
been in 'orrible agony since Sunday.

GEORGE: Where is 'e?

ELLEN: Upstairs in bed.

GEORGE: I'll pop up and see 'im.

ELLEN: He's asleep now.

FLO: 'Ow did 'e come to 'ave the haccident?

MRS. S. (*firmly and with great emphasis*): Cycling, Flo.
He was cycling and 'e fell orf.

FLO: I didn't know 'e 'ad a cycle.

MRS. S.: 'E 'asn't any more.

JANE (*rising*): Well, you will tell him how sorry we
were not to have seen him, won't you? And I do hope
he'll soon be quite well again. Come along, Edward.
We really must go now.

EDWARD (*rising*): All right, Mother.

66

A COCKNEY SCENE ON HAMPSTEAD HEATH.

ELLEN: It was so kind of you, ma'am, to come all this way to see us and to bring Fanny that lovely doll, and everything. Fanny, come and say good-bye to 'er ladyship.

FANNY *makes an abortive effort at a curtsey.*

JANE *bends down and kisses* FANNY.

JANE: Good-bye, Fanny. (*To* MRS. SNAPPER) Good-bye, Mrs. Snapper. (*She shakes hands.*) Good-bye. (*She bows to* FLO *and* GEORGE.)

FLO: Pleased to 'ave made your acquaintance, I'm sure.

JANE (*to* ELLEN): Good-bye, Ellen, it's been delightful seeing you again, and to find you well and happy. Don't fail to remember me to Bridges; my husband and I miss you both still, it seems only yesterday that you were with us.

ELLEN: We miss you, too, ma'am.

JANE: Time changes many things, but it can't change old friends, can it?

ELLEN (*emotionally*): No, ma'am. Oh, no, ma'am.

EDWARD, *who has been saying his good-bye to* MRS. SNAPPER *and* FLO *and* GEORGE, *joins* JANE.

EDWARD: Good-bye, Ellen. Good luck.

ELLEN: Good-bye, Master Edward. Thank you for coming——

JANE *and* EDWARD *are about to leave when the street door bursts open and:*

BRIDGES *staggers into the room. He looks unkempt and unshaven, and is obviously drunk.*

*There is a moment of horrible silence.*

67

BRIDGES *sees* JANE *and* EDWARD *and pulls up short.*

ELLEN (*in agonised tones*): Oh, Alfred!

BRIDGES: Ow! So that's why you wash trying to get me out of the way——

MRS. S.: Alfred Bridges, be'ave yourself and take yer 'at orf.

BRIDGES (*bowing low to* JANE): Pleashed to see you again, milady, I'm shure—welcome to our 'ovel. (*He lurches towards* JANE.)

JANE *makes an instinctive movement away from* BRIDGES.

BRIDGES *draws himself up unsteadily.*

Ow! I shee—proud and 'aughty, are we——

ELLEN (*wildly*): Alfred, stop it! Stop it!

JANE (*suddenly coming forward and taking both* ELLEN'S *hands in hers*): Ellen—dear Ellen—I'm so very, very, sorry, and I quite understand. Please don't be upset and let me come and see you again soon.

JANE *goes out with* EDWARD.

*Again there is silence.*

ELLEN *bursts into hopeless sobbing.*

MRS. S.: You drunken great brute!

BRIDGES: Shut yer mouth. You mind yours and I'll mind mine.

GEORGE: Look 'ere, 'ole man, you'd better come up and 'ave a lie down. (*He takes* BRIDGES' *arm.*)

BRIDGES (*pushing* GEORGE *away*): Leave me alone. Lot of shnobs—that's wot—lot of bloody shnobs. I'm not good enough to be 'ome when the quality comes. Ow, no—we'll see who'sh good enough.

ELLEN (*wailing*): Oh, oh, oh! I'll never be able to raise me 'ead again—never—never——

BRIDGES: 'Oo give Fanny that doll? 'Er noble ladyship?

MRS. S. (*stepping forward*): You let the child alone.

BRIDGES (*pushing* MRS. SNAPPER *so hard that she falls against the table*): I can buy me own child a doll, can't I? Don't want any bloody charity 'ere. (*He snatches the doll from* FANNY *and pitches it into the fire.*)

> FANNY *screams.*
>
> FLO *makes a dart at the fireplace and finally gets the doll out.*
>
> FANNY *continues to scream.*
>
> ELLEN *goes for* BRIDGES.
>
> BRIDGES *hits* ELLEN.
>
> FLO *and* GEORGE *grab* BRIDGES *and push him out of the room.*
>
> ELLEN, *sobbing, takes* FANNY *in her arms.*
>
> MRS. SNAPPER *sinks into a chair.*

ELLEN: She was right—she was right. Time changes many things——

> *The lights fade.*

# SCENE II

*Principals*

FANNY
FLO

FLO CRIES TO ELLEN THAT BRIDGES IS DEAD.

## SCENE II

SCENE: *A London street. The exterior of the public house—
the bar parlour of which was the preceding scene—is
down stage left. There is a street leading away into
darkness up left, and another turning a corner up right.
A wedge of houses separates the two streets. There are
people at most of the windows of the houses. Down
stage right are more houses.*

TIME: *About 10 p.m. Saturday, June 16th, 1906.*

*The centre of the stage is crowded with people and
barrows lit by naphtha flares. There is another pub up
right from which comes the sound of a penny-in-the-slot
piano and the sound of singing and laughter. Everyone is
moving about and talking. Women with caps and shawls
and string bags are shopping at the booths. Some
sailors come out of the left pub with two flashily-dressed
girls and roll across to the pub opposite, into which they
disappear. A policeman walks through the crowd and
goes off. A German band assembles down stage left
and begins to play, effectively drowning the noise of three
Coster youths playing mouth-organs. A few Costers in
pearlies start dancing, a ring is made round them, and
people applaud and yell from the windows. A Salvation
Army Band marches on right and proceeds to play and
sing hymns, against the German band. A few people
make a ring round them and begin singing.*

FANNY *comes out of the pub left and begins to dance by herself.*

*Some of the crowd laugh and those who are dancing stop and applaud her. A Coster darts forward and puts his pearly cap on* FANNY'S *head.*

BRIDGES *comes reeling out of the pub—sees* FANNY, *and tries to grab hold of her. He is prevented by the crowd and*

BRIDGES *is pushed off the stage up right.*

*Suddenly from just where* BRIDGES *has gone there comes a shout and then an agonising scream. The policeman runs across in the direction of the noise. All the crowd, scenting a street accident, surge off, including the German band.*

*Exeunt crowd and German Band.*

FLO *comes flying out of the pub and*

FLO *disappears with the crowd.*

FANNY *continues to dance in pool of light shed by a street lamp, to the rather dismal music of the Salvation Army.*

FLO *comes rushing back and hammers on the door of the pub.*

FLO: Ellen! Ellen! It's Alfred—'e's been run over—'e's dead. Ellen! Ellen!

*The lights fade.*

## SCENE III

*Principals*

EDWARD (aged 21)
JOE (aged 17)
TIM BATEMAN
DOUGLAS FINN
LORD MARTLET (Chubby)
MARION CHRISTIE
NETTA LAKE (pianist)
ROSE DARLING (Ada in "Mirabelle")
CONNIE CRAWSHAY
DAISY DEVON

# SCENE III

SCENE: *Private room in a popular London restaurant. A supper table set for ten is on one side of the stage. There is a sofa up at the back and another down stage right, and an upright piano.*
TIME: *About* 1 *a.m. Wednesday, March* 10*th,* 1909.

Round the table are seated EDWARD (*twenty-one*), TIM BATEMAN, DOUGLAS FINN, MARION CHRISTIE, NETTA LAKE, *and* ROSE DARLING.

*On the sofa up stage in a more or less amorous attitude are seated* LORD MARTLET (Chubby) *and* DAISY DEVON.

*On the down stage sofa is seated* JOE (*aged seventeen*) *with* CONNIE CRAWSHAY, *a very fat blonde.*

*Everyone is very gay. They are all in evening dress. The men in white ties and the women elaborately and slightly theatrically fashionable.*

JOE *is obviously the youngest present and appears well on the way to being very drunk.*

ROSE (*rising, with a glass of champagne in her hand*): I want to propose a toast—to our host!

EVERYONE: Hear, hear! (*Etc.*)

MARION: A lovely little toastie to our lovely little hostie.

77

ROSE: Health, wealth and happiness to our Eddie!

EVERYONE (*repeating*): Health, wealth and happiness! Eddie! (*Etc.*)

> *They clink glasses.*

CONNIE (*to* JOE): Here, sit up. They're drinking your brother's health.

JOE (*rising unsteadily*): Hear, hear—a thousand times hear, hear!

> *They all sing "For he's a jolly good fellow," which tails off into cries for "speech."*

EDWARD (*rising*): Ladies and gentlemen——

JOE (*loudly*): Hurray!

EDWARD: Shut up, Joe.

JOE: I won't shut up. Connie agrees with me, don't you, Connie?

CONNIE: Yes, dear, completely, dear. Shut up, dear.

JOE: Good old Connie. (*He subsides on* CONNIE'S *lap.*)

EDWARD (*continuing*): First of all, in response to your charming toast, I want to apologise for the presence here to-night of my scrubby little brother Joe.

> *Laughter.*

JOE: Here—I say!

> CONNIE *puts her hand over* JOE'S *mouth.*

EDWARD: He is a crawling, loathsome little creature, as you see, and he really ought not to be here at all, but in his little cot at Eton. I felt, however, that as his elder brother, it was my duty to show him how grown-up people behave. Bring him over here, Connie—he must be christened in Clicquot.

CONNIE: He's almost confirmed in it already.

CONNIE *drags* JOE *over to the table where, protesting loudly, he is anointed by* EDWARD *with champagne.*

JOE: I must speak now. I want to speak.

CONNIE: Let him speak, dear, he's having a lovely time.

JOE: Ladies and gentlemen—I have always looked up to my elder brother Edward. He has always been my ideal of what a great big gas-bag should be, and I take this opportunity of asking Connie to marry me.

*Laughter.*

CONNIE: Oh, isn't he sweet!

ROSE: You can't have Connie, Joe, she's married already; you'd better choose me. I'm a widow.

*Everybody chants "The Merry Widow" waltz for a moment.*

JOE: But I love Connie.

CONNIE: Very well, dear, come back to the sofa, dear. (*She leads* JOE *back.*)

EDWARD (*to* LORD MARTLET): Chubby, come out of that corner, you've been there long enough.

DAISY (*coming down*): Quite long enough. This takes me back to the old days of private hansoms. (*She fans herself.*) Give me a drink, somebody.

MARION (*gloomily*): I was once sick in a private hansom.

ROSE: That must have been lovely, dear; tell us about it.

MARION: Well, it was the two hundredth performance of "Floradora."

ROSE: By God, she's going to!

MARION: And they suddenly put me in the sextette without a rehearsal, and I suppose the excitement went to my stomach.

ROSE: I was in "Mirabelle" then, with poor old Laura Marsden.

EDWARD: "Mirabelle"! I was taken to see that. Mother was there on Mafeking night. She took me a few weeks later to a matinée.

MARION: *Taken* to see it, were you! That dates us a bit.

EDWARD: I remember now. You were Ada——

ROSE: Yes, I was Ada.

MARION: And Laura Marsden was Mirabelle, and Mikey Banks was Tom. What a cast that was!

TIM: What happened to Laura Marsden?

ROSE: She died. (*She makes a significant drinking gesture.*)

TIM: Oh, I see.

ROSE: Nine years ago. Give me another drink, or I shall get reminiscent like Marion.

> NETTA *goes over to the pinao and starts thumping the Mirabelle waltz.*

Oh, shut up!

EDWARD: Sing it, Rose.

ROSE: I can't—haven't got any voice.

EVERYONE: Come on, Rose—sing it. Come on, you're among friends.

ROSE: I can't sing it like Laura used to. (*She sings the refrain of the waltz, occasionally forgetting a word or two.*)

80

*Everybody applauds.*

MARION: They do take you back, don't they, those old tunes.

NETTA *strikes up "Keep off the Grass."*

*The girls sing it together.*

*None of the men are really old enough to remember it.*

CHUBBY: Play something we all know.

NETTA *starts "Mary" from "Miss Gibbs."*

*Everyone joins in. They all go into "The Merry Widow" waltz and sing it lustily as*

*The lights fade.*

## SCENE IV

*Principals*

JANE
ROBERT
JOE
MARGARET
ELLEN
FANNY
MRS. SNAPPER
FLO
GEORGE
1ST WOMAN
2ND WOMAN
UNCLE GEORGE
UNCLE DICK

*Daily Mail Photo*

THE MEETING ON THE BEACH OF A POPULAR SEASIDE RESORT.

# SCENE IV

SCENE: *The beach of a popular seaside resort.*
TIME: *About 6 p.m. Monday, July 25th, 1910.*

*The Parade runs along the back about 10 feet above stage level. Down stage left a bandstand on the same level as the Parade juts out on to the beach. On the right the high supports of a swimming enclosure.*

*There are bathing machines and huts and deck chairs— in fact, all the paraphernalia of a popular seaside town in July.*

*The beach is crowded with people, some paddling, some playing games, and a lot clustered round an open-air stage, listening to* UNCLE GEORGE'S *concert party.*

*The Concert Party consists of six men:* UNCLE DICK, UNCLE BOB, UNCLE HARRY, UNCLE JIM, UNCLE JACK *and* UNCLE GEORGE *himself. They are all dressed in straw hats, coloured blazers and rather grubby white flannel trousers.*

*People are constantly passing to and fro along the Parade, and leaning on the railing, looking down on to the beach.*

*When the curtain rises* UNCLE GEORGE *is singing "Put a little bit away for a rainy day." He finishes with a great flourish, then steps forward.*

UNCLE GEORGE: Ladies and gentlemen and kiddies—

85

I am very happy to announce that the winner of this week's Song and Dance Competition is little Miss Fanny Bridges.

*Everyone applauds.*

And it gives me great pleasure to present her with this handsome prize as a souvenir of Uncle George and his merry men. Come on up, my dear.

ELLEN (*in black*) *hoists* FANNY *up from the front row.*

FANNY *is hoisted up by* ELLEN. *She is wearing a white dress with a black sash.*

UNCLE GEORGE *kisses* FANNY *and presents her with a box of chocolates.*

*The audience clap and one little girl is led away yelling, apparently an unsuccessful competitor.*

UNCLE GEORGE: And now, to conclude this programme Uncle Dick will sing "Take me back to Yorkshire."

UNCLE DICK *rises and sings.*

*All the rest join in the chorus, and then, after perfunctory applause, the crowd round the booth disperses.*

UNCLE GEORGE *and his* MERRY MEN *pack up their props and disappear in due course up the steps on to the Parade.*

*Exeunt* UNCLE GEORGE *and his* MERRY MEN.

ELLEN *and* FANNY *walk across the beach with* MRS. SNAPPER, FLO *and* GEORGE. *They meet* MARGARET HARRIS, JANE *and* JOE.

JANE: Why, it can't be—Ellen—what a surprise!

*They shake hands.*

86

ELLEN: Oh, Ma'am—I'd no idea—fancy you being here!

JANE: Margaret, Joe, you remember Ellen, don't you?

MARGARET (*shaking hands*): Of course! yes—how do you do, Ellen?

JOE: Hullo, Ellen.

ELLEN: You remember mother—Mrs. Snapper—and Flo and George, my cousins by marriage?

JANE: Yes, indeed.

MRS. S.: Delighted, I'm sure.

*Everyone shakes hands and talks politely.*

ELLEN: Well, Master Joe, 'ow you 'ave grown. Quite the young man about town! How's Master Edward?

JOE: He's here. He and Edith have been to a concert on the pier. They'll be along soon.

ELLEN (*to* JANE): I got your letter, ma'am, when my Alfred died; it was kind of you to write.

JANE: How is your business going?

ELLEN: Oh, very well, really. I've managed to save quite a bit one way and another, and now I've closed the 'ole place for a month so as to give Fanny a holiday. She goes to dancing school now. She's going on the stage.

MARGARET: Surely she's very young.

MRS. S.: She's set on it—plain set on it.

ROBERT *comes down on to the beach. He has grey hair now and looks very distinguished.*

ROBERT: Jane—there you are—Why, Ellen! (*He shakes hands.*)

*All the introductions start all over again.*

*Two elderly women pass in front of them, talking.*

1ST WOMAN: She went on board the ship dressed as a boy, and that's how the Captain recognised them.

2ND WOMAN: 'Er 'air probably come down under 'er cap.

1ST WOMAN: I don't know 'ow she managed at meals. She couldn't wear 'er cap then.

2ND WOMAN: It's Mrs. Crippen that gets on my mind, poor dear, being all chopped up into little tiny pieces—

*They pass on and up the steps.*

*Meanwhile the* MARRYOTS *and* ELLEN *are parting company.*

ELLEN: It's been lovely seeing you again, ma'am, and you, too, Mrs. Harris. I expect your Edith has grown into a great big girl by now. I remember her when she was ever so small. (*To* ROBERT) Good-bye, sir— good-bye, Master Joe.

ROBERT: Good-bye, Ellen.

JOE: Good-bye.

JANE: You must come and see us one day—bring Fanny to tea.

ELLEN: Thank you, ma'am—I'd like to see the 'ouse again. I was very 'appy there——

*The* MARRYOTS *and* MARGARET *go off.*

MRS. SNAPPER, ELLEN *and* FANNY *rejoin* FLO *and* GEORGE, *who have been standing waiting for them a little way off.*

*The Band, having assembled, breaks into a gay march. A man walks along with a tray of pink rock, yelling.*

88

*All dialogue is drowned in the noise of the band. Several children dodge in and out, playing Tag. One childs falls down and screams. Suddenly there is the noise of an aeroplane. Everyone screams and surges down to the beach, staring upwards. The band stops abruptly and cranes out of the bandstand. People half dressed rush out of bathing machines. Somebody starts cheering—then everyone takes it up. The aeroplane noise grows fainter. The Band strikes up again. A troop of Boy Scouts with a very sour six-piece band march along the Parade. Suddenly there is a roll of thunder. Everyone looks up apprehensively, people on the beach begin to collect their children and belongings. It starts to rain, gently at first, then develops into a down-pour. People put their coat collars up and run. Several umbrellas go up, then more, until the whole beach becomes a sea of umbrellas. Gradually everyone scurries off. The bandstand has by now let down its weather blinds. One fat old woman is left asleep in a deck chair. A tremendous roll of thunder wakes her abruptly and she struggles to get up, and falls back into the chair, which collapses.*

# SCENE V

*Principals*

EDWARD
EDITH

# SCENE V

SCENE: *The deck of an Atlantic liner. This is quite a small inset scene. The rail of the Promenade Deck faces the audience. Behind it can be seen the lighted windows of the lounge. Above can be seen vaguely the Boat Deck, with ventilators and a funnel silhouetted against the stars.*

TIME: *About 7 p.m. Sunday, April 14th, 1912.*

EDWARD *and* EDITH, *he in dinner-jacket, she in evening dress, are leaning on the rail.*

EDITH: It's too big, the Atlantic, isn't it?

EDWARD: Far too big.

EDITH: And too deep.

EDWARD: Much, much too deep.

EDITH: I don't care a bit, do you?

EDWARD: Not a scrap.

EDITH: Wouldn't it be awful if a magician came to us and said: "Unless you count accurately every single fish in the Atlantic you die to-night?"

EDWARD: We should die to-night.

EDITH: How much would you mind—dying, I mean?

EDWARD: I don't know really—a good deal, I expect.

EDITH: I don't believe I should mind so very much now. You see, we could never in our whole lives be happier than we are now, could we?

EDWARD: Darling, there *are* different sorts of happiness.

EDITH: This is the best sort.

EDWARD (*kissing her*): Sweetheart!

EDITH: Don't darling, we don't want any more of the stewards to know we're on our honeymoon.

EDWARD: Why not? It gives them so much vicarious pleasure. Most of them have forgotten what it was like.

EDITH: Are all honeymoons like this?

EDWARD (*firmly*): Exactly.

EDITH: Oh, Edward—that's rather disheartening, isn't it? I do so want this to be unique.

EDWARD: It is, for us.

EDITH: Did you ever think when we were children, going to the pantomime, and going to the Zoo, and playing soldiers, that we should ever be married?

EDWARD: Of course I didn't.

EDITH: Was I nice as a child?

EDWARD: Horrible!

EDITH: So were you, and so was Joe—vile. You always used to take sides against me.

EDWARD: And yet we all liked one another really.

EDITH: I think I liked Joe better than you, but then he was younger and easier to manage. Dear Joe, he was awfully funny at the wedding, wasn't he?

EDWARD: Ribald little beast!

EDITH: He has no reverence, I'm afraid.

EDWARD: Absolutely none.

EDITH: He's passing gallantly through the chorus-girl phase now, isn't he?

THE SINKING "TITANIC": DRAWN BY HENRY REUTERDAHL FROM INFORMATION
SUPPLIED BY A SURVIVOR.

EDWARD: Gallantly but not quickly.

EDITH: Well, darling, you took your time over it.

EDWARD: Now then, Edith——

EDITH: You had several affairs before you married me, didn't you?

EDWARD: Light of my life, shut up!

EDITH: You'd be awfully cross if *I* had, wouldn't you?

EDWARD: Had what?

EDITH: Affairs—love affairs—before you.

EDWARD: Did you?

EDITH: Hundreds.

EDWARD: Liar!

EDITH: I rather wish I had, really. Perhaps I should have learnt some tricks to hold you with when you begin to get tired of me.

EDWARD: I never shall, tricks or no tricks.

EDITH: Yes, you will one day. You're bound to; people always do. This complete loveliness that we feel together now will fade, so many years and the gilt wears off the gingerbread, and just the same as the stewards, we shall have forgotten what it was like.

EDWARD (*seriously*): Answer me one thing, truly, dearest. Have you ever seen gingerbread with gilt on it?

EDITH: Never!

EDWARD: Then the whole argument is disposed of. Anyhow, look at father and mother; they're perfectly happy and devoted, and they always have been.

EDITH: They had a better chance at the beginning. Things weren't changing so swiftly; life wasn't so restless.

EDWARD: How long do you give us?

EDITH: I don't know—and Edward—(*she turns to him*) I don't care. This is our moment—complete and heavenly. I'm not afraid of anything. This is our own, for ever.

EDWARD *takes* EDITH *in his arms and kisses her.*

EDWARD: Do you think a nice warming glass of sherry would make it any more heavenly?

EDITH: You have no soul, darling, but I'm very attached to you. Come on——

EDITH *takes up her cloak which has been hanging over the rail, and they walk away. The cloak has been covering a life-belt, and when it is withdrawn the words "S.S. Titanic" can be seen in black letters on the white.*

*The lights fade into complete darkness, but the letters remain glowing as*

*The orchestra plays very softly and tragically "Nearer My God to Thee."*

# SCENE VI

*Principals*

JANE
ROBERT
JOE
MARGARET

## SCENE VI

SCENE: *The drawing-room of a London house. The room is dark; the blinds are down over the windows.*

TIME: *About 11.16 p.m. Tuesday, August 4th, 1914.*

> *There is the sound of voices outside.*
> *Enter* JANE *and* MARGARET, *both in travelling clothes.*
> JANE *turns on the lights and the room is seen to be enshrouded in dust-sheets.*

JANE (*shuddering*): Why is it that a house that's been shut up for a little while feels so awful? (*She goes to the windows, pulls up the blinds, and opens the windows wide*). There! That's better. It's stifling.     *31981*

MARGARET (*taking off her hat and coat*): That was definitely the most uncomfortable journey I've ever experienced.

> JOE *rushes in. He still has his hat and coat on.*

JOE: Mum, have you got any change? Father and I have both run out.

MARGARET: I have—here—(*she fumbles in her bag*) How much d'you want?

JOE: Four bob.

MARGARET: There's half-a-crown and two shillings.

JOE: Thanks, Aunt Margaret.

> JOE *goes out again.*

JANE: Help me with these dust-sheets, Margaret. Put them anywhere. We'll get a char in to-morrow to clean up.

*They proceed to pull the dust-sheets off the furniture.*

I shall never go on a holiday again, ever. It's horrid when you're there, and much worse when you come back.

MARGARET: Still it's better to be here in London if anything's going to happen.

JANE: It's going to happen all right. I'm afraid there's no doubt about it, now.

MARGARET (*glancing out of the window*): There seem to be lots more people in the streets than usual—where on earth do they all come from?

JOE *comes in, this time without his hat and coat.*

JOE: Well, that's that!

JANE: Where's father?

JOE: Groping about in the wine cellar like an angry old beetle. He says strong drink is essential in a crisis.

JANE: We must have something to eat, too. I wonder if there is anything.

JOE: There's a strong bit of cold tongue in the larder. I just put my head in and it sang the Marseillaise.

JANE: There must be some biscuits, or something.

JANE *goes out hurriedly.*

JOE (*to* MARGARET): Cigarette? (*He offers her his case.*)

MARGARET (*taking one*): Thank you, Joe.

JOE (*lighting them*): This is pretty thrilling, isn't it?

MARGARET: Yes, I suppose so.  I must really go and help Jane.

> MARGARET *runs out, almost colliding with*
> ROBERT, *who is entering with two bottles and some glasses.*

ROBERT: I could only find hock and port, and port's far too heavy  at this time of night; so we'll have to drink to the downfall of Germany in their own damned wine.

JOE: I rather like Germans, don't you, Father?

ROBERT: Enormously.  Move these things off the table, and help me open the bottles.

JOE (*doing so*): Got a corkscrew?

ROBERT: In  my  left  pocket.

> JOE *gropes for the corkscrew while*
> ROBERT *puts the bottles and glasses on the table.*

JOE (*wrestling with a bottle*): If there is a war, how long do you think it will last?

ROBERT: Three months, at the outside.

JOE: I suppose we shall win, shan't we?

ROBERT: Yes—we shall win.

JOE (*hopefully*): Maybe it will last six months.

ROBERT: Leaving everything else aside, that would be economically quite impossible.  Have you any idea of what a war costs, Joe, in actual money?

JOE: Hell of a lot, I should think.

ROBERT: You're quite right.  And the Germans can afford it even less than we can.  And then there's Russia.

JOE: Good old Russia!

ROBERT: And France and Italy and America.

JOE: And Japan and China and Finland—why, by God! we've got 'em licked before we start.

ROBERT: Don't be silly, Joe.

JOE: Are you glad you left the Army, Father, or sorry?

ROBERT: Absolutely delighted.

JOE: Will you go back again?

ROBERT: I expect so.

JOE: How will you feel about that?

ROBERT: Absolutely delighted.

JOE: I suppose I shall have to do something about it, too.

ROBERT: Do you want to?

JOE: Terribly.

ROBERT: Why?

JOE: I don't know. It's—it's sort of exciting, isn't it?

ROBERT: Yes, but don't set your hopes too high, Joey—it takes a lot of training to make a soldier. It will all be over before you get far.

JOE: I wish Edward hadn't been drowned, we could have started off together.

ROBERT (*after a slight pause*): Don't be too impulsive and patriotic and dashing, Joey. Think of your Mother. Think of me, too, you're all we've got left.

ROBERT *abruptly puts down the bottle he is holding and*

ROBERT *goes out on to balcony.*

JOE *stands staring after* ROBERT *thoughtfully.*

JANE *enters carrying a tray.*

KITCHENER'S MEN IN 1914.

MARGARET *enters following* JANE, *with some plates.*

JANE: We found some potted meat and biscuits and Worcester Sauce; and the tongue doesn't look too bad.

JOE (*taking the tray from* JANE): It isn't its looks I object to, it's its personality.

JOE *puts the tray on the table.*

*A newsboy runs by outside shouting.*

ROBERT *shouts from the balcony and goes hurriedly from the room.*

JOE, JANE *and* MARGARET *stand stock still, waiting.*

ROBERT *returns with the paper.*

ROBERT: We're at war, my dears.

JOE (*grabbing the paper*): Let me see—let me see——

MARGARET: Listen—listen!

*From far away comes the sound of cheering.*

MARGARET *runs out on the balcony for a moment, and then returns.*

JANE *sinks down on a chair.*

JANE: It's very hot, isn't it?

JOE: Don't look sad, mum. It won't last long; Father says it can't possibly; and it's terribly exciting.

JANE: I didn't mean to look sad; I feel rather tired.

JOE (*handing* JANE *a glass of wine*): Here, mum dear— have a nice sozzle. We ought all to get drunk really, and go roaring about the streets——

JANE: Edward missed this, anyhow. At least he died when he was happy, before the world broke over his head.

ROBERT: Don't take that view, dearest, it's foolish.

We've had wars before without the world breaking.

JANE: My world isn't very big.

*A group of people pass along under the balcony laughing and cheering. Some of them start singing the Marseillaise and the others drown them with Rule Britannia.*

JANE *gets up suddenly.*

JANE: Drink to the war, then, if you want to. I'm not going to. I can't! Rule Britannia! Send us victorious, happy and glorious! Drink, Joey, you're only a baby, still, but you're old enough for war. Drink like the Germans are drinking, to Victory and Defeat, and stupid, tragic sorrow. But leave me out of it, please!

JANE *goes abruptly from the room.*

*The lights fade.*

## SCENE VII

*Above the proscenium* 1914 *glows in lights. It changes to*
1915-1916, 1917 *and* 1918. *Meanwhile, soldiers march*
*uphill endlessly. Out of darkness into darkness.*
*Sometimes they sing gay songs, sometimes they whistle,*
*sometimes they march silently, but the sound of their*
*tramping feet is unceasing. Below, the vision of them*
*brightly-dressed, energetic women appear in pools of*
*light, singing stirring recruiting songs—"Sunday I walk*
*out with a soldier," "We don't want to lose you," etc.,*
*etc. With* 1918 *they fade away, as also does the vision of*
*the soldiers, although the soldiers can still be heard very*
*far off, marching and singing their songs.*

# SCENE VIII

*Principals*

JOE
FANNY

# SCENE VIII

SCENE: *A restaurant.*

TIME: *About 7.30 p.m. Tuesday, October 22nd, 1918.*

    JOE *and* FANNY *are seated at a table; they have just finished dinner.*

    JOE *is in officer's uniform.*

    FANNY *is in very charming day clothes. She is now nineteen and extremely attractive.*

JOE (*pouring some champagne into* FANNY's *glass*): Have some more.

FANNY: Darling, I shall be tight. You don't want me to fall down during my first number, do you?

JOE: How much do you love me?

FANNY: Now, then, dear, we've had all this out before.

JOE: Will you send me a telegram to Dover?

FANNY: Of course I will. I promised, didn't I?

JOE: Once you get into the theatre, with all those changes, you might forget.

FANNY: I'll send Maggie out with it.

JOE: Dear old Maggie. Say good-bye to her for me, won't you?

FANNY: Aren't you coming down to talk to me while I make up?

JOE: No, I promised to go home. Mother's waiting for me.

FANNY: I shall have to give it to you now, then.

JOE: What?

FANNY: Just a little something I had made for you.

JOE: Oh, Fanny—what is it?

FANNY: Hold on a minute, dear. It's in my bag.

*She searches in her bag and produces a small packet.*
Here—with my love.

JOE (*opening it*): Oh, it's lovely.

FANNY: It's nothing really. Just a little souvenir of
all the fun we've had.

JOE: You are a darling!

FANNY (*grabbing it from* JOE): Here, silly, you've
missed the whole point. It opens—there.

FANNY *opens the little locket and discloses a minute*
*photograph of herself.*

JOE (*taking it*): It will be with me always, to the end
of my days.

FANNY: You won't want it that long.

JOE: I almost wish I didn't love you quite so awfully.
It makes going back much worse.

FANNY: I shall miss you dreadfully.

JOE: It has been fun, hasn't it?

FANNY: Lovely.

JOE: You don't regret it—any of it?

FANNY: Not a moment of it.

JOE: How wonderful you are. Do you really love
me, I wonder, deep down inside, I mean?

FANNY: Yes, I think so.

JOE: Enough to marry me?

FANNY: Yes, but I wouldn't.

JOE: Why not?

FANNY: It would be too difficult. We shouldn't be happy married. Your Mother wouldn't like it.

JOE: She'd be all right.

FANNY: Don't let's talk about it now. Let's wait until you come back.

JOE: Very well.

*There is silence for a moment.*

FANNY *puts her hand on* JOE's *across the table.*

FANNY: Listen, dear. I love you and you love me, and I've got to go now or I shall be late; and you've got to go, too, but I'm not going to say good-bye. We've had fun, grand fun, and I don't want you to forget me, that's why I gave you the locket. Please keep it close to you, Joey—darling Joey.

FANNY *goes as*

*The lights fade.*

# SCENE IX

*Principals*

JANE
JOE

*Stage Photo Company*

THE "LEAVE" TRAIN IN VICTORIA STATION DURING THE WAR.

# SCENE IX

SCENE: *A railway station. The station is foggy and very dimly lit on account of air raids. The ticket barrier can be vaguely discerned and beyond it, the back of a train. Just above the barrier a lamp shines downwards partially illuminating a recruiting poster. On the right is an empty platform, but there are people moving about on it, and several Red Cross orderlies and nurses. There is a crowd of people, mostly women, clustered around the left barrier—occasionally a door in the train opens and a shaft of light falls on to the platform.*

TIME: *About 11 p.m. Tuesday, October 22nd, 1918.*

*A crowd of soldiers comes on from the left, wearing full equipment. They are greeted by some of the women. Presently a Sergeant enters, and after their good-byes have been said, the Sergeant gets them in line and marches them through on to the platform, where they can be seen getting into the train.*

*JANE and JOE come on from the left.*

JOE (*breathlessly*): Whew: I thought we were going to miss it, didn't you, mum?

JANE: Yes.

JOE: Not much time for long good-byes, darling.

JANE: I know. I'm glad, really—aren't you?

JOE: Yes. I never know what to say.

JANE: I'm almost hardened to it by now. This has happened so often.

JOE: Dearest mum, you are marvellous. You never make a fuss.

JANE: Don't be too sweet to me, Joey, I don't want to disgrace you, to behave badly.

JOE: You couldn't behave badly.

JANE: How funny! Do you know that Robert said that to me years and years ago. I must be very dull and unimaginative to be so reserved. It was the Boer War, then. This is very, very different.

*A whistle blows.*

JOE *takes* JANE *in his arms.*

JOE: Good-bye, darling.

JANE: Good-bye, darling—take care of yourself.

*JOE rushes through the barrier and jumps into the train just as it starts to move.*

*JANE stands under the lamp looking after him.*

*Two or three of the women at the barrier burst into loud sobbing, some soldiers in the train start singing. A big steaming locomotive comes slowly to a standstill at the right hand platform. Almost immediately Red Cross Orderlies begin to walk off the platform carrying wounded men on stretchers.*

*JANE stands watching them; her face is quite expressionless. Then with a trembling hand she takes a cigarette out of her bag and lights it.*

*The lights fade.*

## SCENE X

*Principals*

JANE
ELLEN
GLADYS (A parlourmaid)

# SCENE X

SCENE: *The drawing-room of a London house. The decoration of the room has changed slightly with the years, but not to any marked extent. It looks very much the same as it has always looked.*
TIME: *About 11 a.m. Monday, November 11th, 1918.*

*As the lights go up on the scene, a* PARLOURMAID *shows* ELLEN *into the room.* ELLEN *has certainly changed with the years. She is very well dressed, almost smart.*

GLADYS: Her Ladyship will be down in a moment, madam.

ELLEN: Thanks.

GLADYS *goes out.*

ELLEN *wanders about the room. There is a photograph of* EDWARD *on the table, and also one of* JOE. *She looks at them both and sighs.*

JANE *enters. She is dressed in street clothes.*

JANE: Ellen! Gladys said Mrs. Bridges, but I couldn't believe it was you.

ELLEN: I just thought I'd call. It's rather important, as a matter of fact.

JANE: Do sit down. I'm delighted to see you again.

ELLEN: Thanks. (*She sits down.*)

JANE: How's Fanny?

ELLEN: Oh, very well. She's in "Over the Moon," now, you know.

JANE: Yes. I went the other night. She was splendid, I felt very proud to know her.

ELLEN: It's about her I've come to see you, really.

JANE: Oh! Well?

ELLEN: It's—it's—er—rather difficult.

JANE: What is it? What on earth is the matter?

ELLEN: About her and Master—her and Joe.

JANE: Joe?

ELLEN: Yes. They've been—well—er—to put it frankly, if you know what I mean, they've been having an affair.

JANE: My Joe?

ELLEN: Yes—your Joe. His last two leaves he spent a lot of time with Fanny.

JANE (*slowly*): Oh, I see.

ELLEN: I wouldn't have come to see you about it at all, only I think Fanny's very upset about it, and now that the war's over—or almost over, that is—and he'll be coming home—I thought——

JANE (*coldly*): What did you think?

ELLEN: Well, I thought they ought to get married.

JANE: Does Fanny want to marry him?

ELLEN: No—er—not exactly. That is—I haven't talked about it to her. She doesn't know I know.

JANE: How do you know?

ELLEN: I found a letter from him——

JANE: And you read it?

CHEERING THE NEWS OF THE ARMISTICE AT THE FRONT ON
NOVEMBER 11TH, 1918.

ELLEN: Yes—it's here. I've brought it with me.
(*She fumbles in her bag.*)

JANE: I don't wish to see it, thank you.

ELLEN: I only brought it because——

JANE (*cutting* ELLEN *short*): Is Fanny in any sort of
trouble?

ELLEN: Oh, no. Nothing like that.

JANE (*rising*): Then I think we'd better leave it until
Joe comes home. Then he and Fanny can decide what
they wish to do.

ELLEN (*also rising*): I—I didn't mean to upset you.

JANE: I'm not in the least upset.

ELLEN: It's been on my mind—it's been worrying
me to death.

JANE: I think you should have spoken to Fanny
before you came to me. I never interfere with my son's
affairs.

ELLEN: Well, I'm sure I'm very sorry.

JANE: Please don't let's discuss it any further.
Good-bye, Ellen.

ELLEN: I suppose you imagine my daughter isn't
good enough to marry your son; if that's the case I can
assure you you're very much mistaken. Fanny's
received everywhere; she knows all the best people.

JANE: How nice for her; I wish I did.

ELLEN: Things aren't what they used to be, you
know—it's all changing.

JANE: Yes, I see it is.

ELLEN: Fanny's at the top of the tree now; she's
having the most wonderful offers.

JANE: Oh, Ellen!

ELLEN: What is it?

JANE: I'm so very, very sorry.

ELLEN: I don't know what you mean.

JANE: Yes, you do—inside, you must. Something seems to have gone out of all of us, and I'm not sure I like what's left. Good-bye, Ellen.

> GLADYS *enters with a telegram.*
>
> JANE *takes telegram.*

Excuse me, will you. (*She opens it and reads it, and then says in a dead voice.*) There's no answer, Gladys.

GLADYS (*excitedly*): It's all over milady—it's eleven o'clock—the maroons are going off.

JANE: Thank you, Gladys, that will do.

GLADYS: Yes, milady.

> GLADYS *goes out.*
>
> JANE *stands holding the telegram. She sways slightly.*

ELLEN: What is it? What's happened? Oh, my God!

JANE: You needn't worry about Fanny and Joe any more, Ellen. He won't be able to come back after all because he's dead. (*She crumples up and falls to the ground.*)

> *Maroons can be heard in the distance and people cheering.*
>
> *The lights fade.*

## SCENE XI

*Principal*

JANE

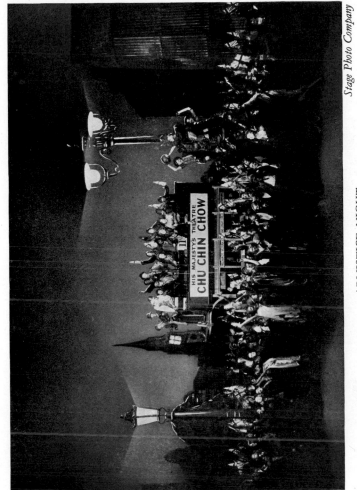

ARMISTICE NIGHT.

*Topical Press*

A TYPICAL SCENE ON ARMISTICE DAY IN LONDON.

## SCENE XI

SCENE: *Trafalgar Square.*
TIME: *11 p.m. Monday, November 11th, 1918.*

*Before the scene begins* JANE *appears far up stage in a pool of light. Her hat has been pushed on to one side, her clothes look dishevelled, and her handbag hangs on her arm wide open. Twined round her neck and over her hat are coloured paper streamers. She holds in her left hand a large painted wooden rattle, in her right hand a red, white and blue paper squeaker. Her face is dead white and quite devoid of expression.*

*The lights go up.*

JANE *can be seen threading her way like a sleep-walker through dense crowds of cheering, yelling people. They push her and jostle her. One man blows a long squeaking paper tongue into her face. There is a motor bus festooned with people and a Rolls Royce and one or two taxis and a hansom cab, all equally burdened with screaming humanity. They move at a snail's pace.* JANE *finally arrives down stage under a lamp-post in the centre. She stands there cheering wildly, with the tears rolling down her face. The lights dim and the yelling crowds fade away.* JANE *is left, still cheering and occasionally brandishing the rattle and blowing the squeaker. But she can't be heard at all because the full strength of the orchestra is playing "Land of Hope and Glory."*

END OF PART II

PART III

# SCENE I

*Principals*

ROBERT
JANE
MARGARET

# SCENE I

Scene: *Drawing-room of a London house.*
Time: 11.45 *p.m. Tuesday, December 31st, 1929.*

> Margaret *and* Jane, *both old women, are sitting
> by the fire.* Margaret *is very made up, with dyed
> hair.* Jane's *hair is white.* Margaret *is wearing a
> coloured evening gown.* Jane *is in black.*

Margaret: I assure you he's the most marvellous
man I've ever met. I'd never go to another doctor in the
world. He has the most wonderful touch—he's
completely cured me, and anyhow the hotel is divine.
It's really more a Hydro really, although, thank God,
not in the English sense. You can eat what you like and
do what you like——

Jane: And what do you like?

Margaret (*laughing*): Enjoying myself.

Jane: And you do.

Margaret: Certainly I do.

Jane: Good!

Margaret: Jane, dear, you really are hopeless.

Jane: I refuse to be jostled, Margaret. I'm perfectly
comfortable where I am, without going gallivanting
about the Continent taking cures for ailments I haven't
got.

Margaret: How do you know you haven't got any
ailments?

JANE: Because I'm sane and active, and as strong as a horse. So is Robert. We've both outstayed our welcome, that's the only thing that's wrong with us.

MARGARET: I don't see any sense in sitting waiting for the grave.

JANE: I'm not waiting for anything. I have a perfectly good time. You're not the only one who enjoys yourself. I go to the Opera. I go to theatres, I go to the Zoo, and, I must say, so far I've found the Zoo infinitely the most entertaining.

MARGARET: Dearest Jane—you really are amazing!

ROBERT *enters. His hair is also white, but he is otherwise hale and hearty.*

ROBERT: It's nearly time.

MARGARET: Good heavens, I must fly. I wouldn't interfere with your little ritual for the world.

JANE: You wouldn't interfere—you're an old friend.

MARGARET (*kissing* JANE): That's very sweet, Jane, but all the same I must go. I promised I'd be at the Embassy at eleven-thirty. Good night, dear. Good night, Robert. No, don't see me down—the car's outside, isn't it?

ROBERT: Yes, it's been there for a long while.

MARGARET: Happy New Year to you both. Remember you're both dining with me on Thursday.

ROBERT: Good night, Margaret—same to you.

MARGARET *goes out.*

ROBERT *goes over to* JANE.

Did Franklin bring the champagne up?

JANE: Yes, it's by the table.

ROBERT: Good!

JANE: Well, Robert—here we go again.

ROBERT: I believe you laugh at me inside—for my annual sentimental outburst.

JANE: No dear, I don't laugh at you.

ROBERT: One more year behind us.

JANE: One more year before us.

ROBERT: Do you mind?

JANE: Oh, no—everything passes—even time.

ROBERT: It seems incredible, doesn't it? Here we are in this same room!

JANE: Yes. I've hated it for years.

ROBERT: Do you want to move?

JANE: Of course not.

ROBERT: We might have some new curtains.

JANE: We have, dear.

ROBERT: Good God, so we have! I never noticed.

JANE: They've only been up a week.

ROBERT: They look very nice.

JANE: Dear Robert. (*She pats* ROBERT'S *hand.*) What toast have you in mind for to-night—something gay and original, I hope?

ROBERT: Just our old friend—the future. The Future of England.

JANE: It's starting—the champagne, quick!

  ROBERT *gets a champagne bottle out of the bucket and struggles with it.*

  JANE *opens the window.*

ROBERT: I can't get the damned thing open.

JANE: Let me try.

ROBERT (*doing it*): There!
> JANE *holds the glasses.*
> ROBERT *fills the glasses.*
> *Meanwhile the chimes and sirens are beginning outside.*

JANE (*holding up her glass*): First of all, my dear, I drink to you. Loyal and loving always. (*She drinks.*) Now, then, let's couple the Future of England with the past of England. The glories and victories and triumphs that are over, and the sorrows that are over, too. Let's drink to our sons who made part of the pattern and to our hearts that died with them. Let's drink to the spirit of gallantry and courage that made a strange Heaven out of unbelievable Hell, and let's drink to the hope that one day this country of ours, which we love so much, will find dignity and greatness and peace again.

> *They both lift their glasses and drink as*
> *The lights fade.*

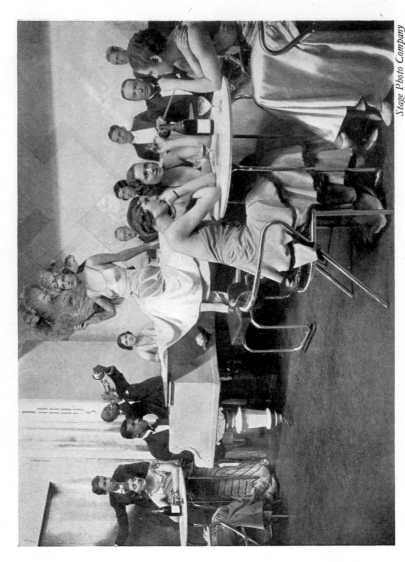

FANNY SINGS OF "THOSE TWENTIETH CENTURY BLUES."

# SCENE II

*Principals*

ROBERT
JANE
FANNY
MARGARET
ELLEN
FULL COMPANY

THE GROUP OF BLIND SOLDIERS BASKET-MAKING IN THE FINAL SCENE OF THE PLAY

"THE —— WORLD'S GONE BROKE."

## SCENE II

SCENE: *A Night Club.*
TIME: *Evening—1930.*
    *This Scene begins with a night club in which* FANNY
*is singing, seated on a piano. The decoration is angular
and strange, and the song she is singing is oddly dis-
cordant.*

## TWENTIETH CENTURY BLUES

### VERSE

Why is it that civilised humanity
Must make the world so wrong?
In this hurly burly of insanity
Your dreams cannot last long.
We've reached a headline—
The Press headline—every sorrow,
Blues value is News value to-morrow.

### REFRAIN

Blues, Twentieth Century Blues, are getting me down.
Who's escaped those weary Twentieth Century Blues.
Why, if there's a God in the sky, why shouldn't he grin?
High above this dreary Twentieth Century din,

In this strange illusion,
Chaos and confusion,
People seem to lose their way.
What is there to strive for,
Love or keep alive for?  Say—
Hey, hey, call it a day.
Blues, nothing to win or to lose.
It's getting me down.
Blues, I've got those weary Twentieth Century Blues.

*When the song is finished, people rise from table and dance without apparently any particular enjoyment; it is the dull dancing of habit. The lights fade away from everything but the dancers, who appear to be rising in the air. They disappear and down stage left six "incurables" in blue hospital uniform are sitting making baskets. They disappear and* FANNY *is seen singing her song for a moment, then far away up stage a jazz band is seen playing wildly. Then down stage* JANE *and* ROBERT *standing with glasses of champagne held aloft, then* ELLEN *sitting in front of a Radio loud speaker; then* MARGARET *dancing with a young man. The visions are repeated quicker and quicker, while across the darkness runs a Riley light sign spelling out news. Noise grows louder and louder. Steam rivets, loud speakers, jazz bands, aeroplane propellers, etc., until the general effect is complete chaos.*

*Suddenly it all fades into darkness and silence and away at the back a Union Jack glows through the blackness.*

138

*The lights slowly come up and the whole stage is composed of massive tiers, upon which stand the entire Company. The Union Jack flies over their heads as they sing "God Save the King."*

THE END